THE STRANGE ATTRACTOR

THE STRANGE ATTRACTOR

NEW AND SELECTED POEMS

Robert Morgan

LOUISIANA STATE UNIVERSITY PRESS   BATON ROUGE   2004

DESIGNER: Amanda McDonald Scallan
TYPEFACE: Sabon
PRINTER AND BINDER: Thomson-Shore, Inc.

Library of Congress Cataloging-in-Publication Data:

Morgan, Robert, 1944–
  The strange attractor : new and selected
poems / Robert Morgan.
    p. cm.
  ISBN 0-8071-2951-8 (alk. paper) —
  ISBN 0-8071-2952-6 (pbk. : alk. paper)
    I. Title.
  PS3563.O87147S87 2004
  811'.54 — dc22

                          2003020200

Zirconia Poems was first published by Lillabulero
Press. *Red Owl* was first published by W. W. Nor-
ton. *Land Diving* was first published by Louisiana
State University Press. *Trunk and Thicket* was first
published by L'Epervier Press. *Groundwork* was
first published by Gnomon Press. *At the Edge of
the Orchard Country* was first published by Wes-
leyan University Press. *Sigodlin* was first published
by Wesleyan University Press. *Green River* was
first published by Wesleyan University Press. *Top-
soil Road* was first published by Louisiana State
University Press. Previously uncollected poems
have appeared in *Appalachian Journal, Blink,
Carolina Quarterly, Counterpoint, Mossy Creek
Journal, New Mexico Humanities Review, Pem-
broke Magazine, Pivot, Rattapallax,* and *Shenan-
doah.*

The author wishes to thank Michael Mcfee and
Robert West for their crucial help in selecting and
editing this volume.

CONTENTS

NEW POEMS

Under Cover

We do not talk loud in forests.
It seems an affront to biggest
trees to shout there, as if we might
disturb their dignity, intrude
on the cool privacy and mood.
It's scary to stand under
such mighty figures with a hunter's
instinct not to warn what lurks there
you're coming. Something in the blood
says don't violate the poise of wood
and wild, don't insult with words
this place where every bush may hide
an ambush, and each syllable
be heard by hidden, larger presence.

Fasting

Nothing is delicious as absence.
The green tracts of tree and hill are read out
and snatched away. The little pindar in
the grass chirps light and night at once.

To feast on nothing, to feast on time
itself, to savor course after course and
lavish after lavish of cool thinning
abstinence in open space thrills welcome

to flesh and colors the air with crystal
and northern lights. High winds in a quartz
are medicine. Nothing satisfies like
nothing. We go fast and faster through all

the sad algorithm of human experience.
We feast on stillness. We wait for new
fevers and feed the fire of air only
to harvest the colors of abundance.

We wake to the old scents of fingernail
and lip, infections of the breath. We soar
into the higher stillness and thrill to
jet streams and dust clouds and whisper chill

in the whisper gallery of distance.
Such are the covert private habits
of hunger, fast awake throughout
history, delicious as absence.

Triolet

In the beginning was the word
breathed from the first body,
that puff of lit gas the stars heard
in the beginning. Was the word
a stream carrying its syllable, a bird
or spark shot through the mind of nobody
in the beginning? Was the word
breathed from the first, body?

Natural Radio

If you turn on a set way back
in the remotest section of
a wilderness, the voices are
astounding. Hear the signals from
electric currents in the earth,
magnetic wells and fountains, storms
of northern lights and southern lights.
You catch the whistle of a bolt,
shriek of lightning, chatter of
auroras. Birds are calling to
each other from the nests of atoms.
Emissions from the surface of
the sun come in as trills. But listen
to the hum of older spaces,
a hush of the beginning worlds,
as steady as tall water on
a mountain's rocky lip, that
speaks of time and matter's first motet.

Wrecking Bar

How heavy is this question mark?
The head is split and tapered to
a forked tongue that loosens seams
and pulls out nails like roots and stitches.
The shaft's octagonal like a gun.
But with the cold steel shepherd's crook
you can explode a mighty house
one nail and joist, one stick and rafter,
one louver at a time. Each nail
drawn out groans why and why and why.
This instrument dissects the work
of ancient carpenters and frees
the bonds of old-time joining.
A simple question mark applied
again, again, evaporates
the fabric's figure. The crozier
inverted excommunicates
components of the whole and leaves
the rubble of sad questioning.

Funny Books

Because my parents had denied
me comic books as sordid and
salacious, I would sneak a look
at those of friends, the bold and bright
slick covers, pages rough as news
and inked in pinks and greens and blues
as cowboys shouted in balloons
and Indian yells were printed on
the clouds. I borrowed books and hid
them in the crib and under shoes
and under bed. The glories of
those hyperbolic zaps and screams
were my illuminated texts,
the chapbook prophets of forbidden
and secret art, the narratives
of quest and conquest in the West,
of Superman and Lash Larue.
The print and pictures cruder than
the catalog were sweeter than
the cake at Bible School. I crouched
in almost dark and swilled the words
that soared in their balloons and bulbs
of grainy breath into my pulse,
into the stratosphere of my
imagination, reaching Mach
and orbit speed, escape velocity
just at the edge of Sputnik's age,
in stained glass windows of the page.

Family

The cricket my familiar,
melodic as a little bird,
has flicked its way downstairs and past
the furnace, scattered toys, junk,
past freezer, to my study. Bright
as a watermelon seed it
hides forgotten and silent
until suddenly while I read
it strikes black sparks from its flint
so pure and unaccompanied
I seem to hear a molecule
of very earth voice its crystal
wet with first fire and pure as
first sleep, cuddled in the planet's
swing and making all familiar.

Signal Corps

Wants someone else to talk to, wants
not to be alone on this
resplendent crust,
among the spooky atoms and

galleries of space.
Curious beyond light years and
the bodiless would
gather round the instant

in communion with some
fleshless voice. Would create
in its own
image an alien

creator, mind ashamed
of its body
that dies, and tired of squatting,
but grateful for a face and tongue.

Legends

for the Thomas Wolfe Centennial

In a distant mountain graveyard
under dusty webs of starlight,
this lone angel points a finger
at the wink of distant galaxies,
stone wrist slender as a flute note.
Who is this that lurks among the
tilted tombstones, forehead beaded,
eyes like snails or glowing mushrooms?
Crickets ping their chisels in the
dewlight; katydids are raging.
Who is this that reads the legends,
these inscriptions, giant carving
lifetimes with a pencil on a
tablet gleaming timeless, glimmering?
From the ghostly page of stone script
spills a thread of foxfire language,
spins a strand of singing tautness
reaching over weed and marker,
stretching over tree and hilltop,
rolling over cliff and hollow,
washing into branch and creekbed,
gathering toward the peopled valleys,
sweeping toward the shivering cities,
strong as the Atlantic river,
flood of names and bawl of freight trains,
soaring trestles, plunging tunnels,
rising in a rage to join all
sentences with mighty ocean,
past the mystery wall of mountains,
sung from spark of angel's finger,
new millennium, century later.

The Strange Attractor

Somewhere out in the reach of space
unseen, as yet unheard, unplaced,
a great mass looms invisible
among the stars and dust spirals
of our decaying and many
mansioned world, so large a body
it twists trajectories and warps
light, stretching orbit and ellipse,
but cannot be found. Yet it's so vast
the galaxies, indeed the rest
of matter, are just fleas to its
shaggy celestial dogness,
still unproved, unrecognized but
by implication, substantiate
only in attraction of lesser
bodies to the unknown greater,
toward a heart that holds the spinning
bits of glitter of the seen in
their coherent scatter, this far
out but not dissolving further
toward nothingness. And it's our
gravity that tells us it is there.

Time's Music

Insects in an August field seem
to register the background noise
of space and amplify the twitch
of partners in atoms. The click
of little timepieces, chirp of
tiny chisels, as grasshoppers
and crickets effervesce and spread
in the weeds ahead, then wash back
in a wake of crackling music
that sparkles through grass, ticking
away the summer, whispering of
frost and stars overhead and chatter
of memory in every bit
of matter, of half-life in
the thick and flick of creation.

Trophy

The sailfish on the wall above the door
of Doctor Fortescue's reception room
was arced forever at the summit of
its leap. While waiting for the test or shot,
the doctor's probing touch and frown, I watched
the great fin soar and hang. The sail was ribbed,
extended like a fan that sawed the air.
I puzzled on the link between the fish
and medicine. The trophy showed the doc
had traveled to the tropics, trolled the deep.
But was the arcing bolt of blue a sign
also of some mysterious tie between
the art of healing and the secret depths?
Or was the monster stuffed a symbol of
the power of knowledge over floods and drowning?
I studied the sleek prize's needle lip
and steeled myself to face the certain dart.

Rhymer Spring

for Kenneth Youngblood

This fountain is so deep and bold
it seems to be an oracle
from underneath the rock and moss
and ferns, reciting poetry
or maybe quoting Scripture to
its hidden mountain pasture. Hear
the stir of inlets whispering where
the dancing sand shows inspiration
of water summoned through the veins
from far in rock and tasting cold
as quartz and metals passed through. See
spring lizards grip the sandy floor
where milk and butter were kept chilled
for longer than a century.
The rim stones make the edges firm
and hold back washing leaves and mud.
The water seems to have a secret
told only to the tongue that drinks.
The current from so deep in earth
will never freeze on blizzard night,
is always cold at hottest noon.
Who tastes this nugget toasts the calm
Bear Wallow Mountain wilderness,
a tract of forest eaten back
by acid of development
around the mountain's plunging robes.
Up here the spring still speaks
of lonely cove and mountain peaks,
and rhymes with clearest winter sky
and glitters with the farthest star,
but hints of driest prophecy.

Church Dust

The oldest wooden churches have
a sediment between the planks
of floor and altar, under pews,
a stive so fine it soaks into
the grain, or flies away before
the broom can touch it to the lip
of pan. The dry mist wrestles in
a beam of light, a shiver dance
that shows the air is troubled in
the stillest house, the quietest room.
The salts and silts from human hope
and human sweat and human mourning,
the bits of hair and flakes of skin,
wash up in corners, lodge in cracks
until a passing step or breath
of weather stirs them up again,
and pieces swirl away like words
from long-forgotten sermons, hymns
once raised at hot revival's end.
A spider works its artistry
beneath the pulpit catching flies.
A mouse hunts through the must for crumbs
beneath the service table, finds
a feast of consecrated lint,
a hornet like a bullet spent,
as time goes cooly counting dust.

ZIRCONIA POEMS (1969)

High County

In the hills, dead springs, blue flame of sky.
The horizon goes all the way around.

When it comes the darkness sprouts from rocks and fills
the valley with wine. Splinters of ice form in the sky,
cold air stoking light.

A crystal trills at the bottom of a well
blasting tunnels upward.

It is the blue sun rising all night under the sea.

From a Cliff

Looking down through electric chairs of space.
Distance, a hot dry mouth, opens,
sucks me to its roots
of frost. Winds the clock inside that yells, Jump,
crush the arms of gravity.

Water Tanks

The water tanks in South Carolina walk
like robots against the sky, bigger than the windmills
or firelookouts along the horizon
of filing black pines. Gray featureless heads rising
over factories and staring twenty miles through haze and over
mud cushioned creek bottoms
to another with another textile name for eyes
and mouth and lightning
needles thin as the radio transmitters to the north for ears
to hear the long overcast boredom
of Sundays, and cars going by and by and by.

They sneak around behind and follow
for miles, shrinking in the mirror to hot black pins,
old truck cabs looking down
on gullies and volcanoes of sawdust.
They rise like buds of junk out of kudzu,
high above white wagonwheels at driveways.
The water tanks look on
like aluminum skulls, graffiti
hung from the mossy sky.

Beginning

Mollusks of snow behind cedars.
The darkness inside trees flows out, river
launching birds of fire.
The pools wear a skin of ice,
hold a leaf corpse near the surface.
A crow punctures distance.
After days of silence
pines
roar their blackness at the fields.

Elegy

Guess I'll light a rag out of here, he said
and blindness rose in his open eyes.

Tilted chessmen, tombstones graze on the hill,
drag shadows at the setting moon.
Eighty years go down

like a ship.

Zirconia

Blue as mildew mountains break beyond the town
and shadows swim the valley.
Now filled with leaves the zircon mines
bleed dirt into the lake.
Further up, the millpond is a brain of mud
and high in the bones of a chestnut
crows watch the town
until the moon lights
the country like a TV screen.

Prayer Meeting

A bonfire lights the faces, and the Greek
from Memphis sings and beats a tambourine, while his daughter
speaks in tongues, dances in the aisles.
Everyone screams, stamps, or waves
his handkerchief and cries.

Except the children who creep into the shadows
to watch, metal hardening in their eyes. A bitter honey
smears the wool of their minds.
Red salamanders crawl out of the moss. Their mothers
unpin their hair and reel with happiness.
The children watch, expressionless as blind men.

Long Beach

Far out surfers rise and die, soar beyond
the lace of foam like gulls, sea buckling under impact;
its tongues smooth and carve the sand.
Dune grass goosesteps under wind.
The ocean is a mountain range of water. The pier
crawls on its back like a centipede
and clouds eddy,
building sierras to the south.
I watch waves gnaw in the jewelry of light,
lunge in and crumble into feathers where the beach
shines like marble, honing the sea
to cut the dunes, retake a continent.

RED OWL (1972)

Cellar

The air moves as if something just left.
Snake breath.
Cool razors circulate
touching the skin with wet silk.
Breathing clear cheese.
Mold flowers grow like plastered snowballs
on the walls, rust-lacquered pipes.
The heads of translucent shoots crawl out of the potato bin
and run like wires to the window.
Once cut straight and firm
the walls have dripped and rotted to black jelly.
Jam grows blue fur.
The light bulb flickers as if circled by moths
fanning its coolness
and lighting on my neck.
Walls sweating mercury, straining
to the weight.

Resin

The pine is smeared with salves,
has thick scabs
and dripping sores.
The spinal fluid runs out
thickening a pouch around itself.
Reddish milk festers
from knotholes
hardening to quartz.
Boiled its spirits return
as oil, an intelligence,
colorless, volatile,
vehicle of color and solvent.
A whiff burns.
But the pine's sweet
blisters balm the air.

White Pines

Standing beneath huge pilings.
Up there where the sea broke, browsed along the sand
millions of years ago.
A faint surf breaks far overhead.

Hog-Wire Fence

Rust mortar still
holds a few bricks of air,
but the net seining others from
property and holding it in from the continuing
terrain is ruptured
and hard to find among the weeds
as a century-old deed in the courthouse.
Disappears turning over like a Möbius strip.
Runs through the middle of trees.
Otherwise the fence holds up
its rotting posts.
The tennis of ownership is played elsewhere.

Whippoorwill

The dead call at sundown from their places
on the mountain and down by the old mill.
They rise from the cellars of trees
and move up and down the valley
all night grazing like deer.
The call:
a rusty windmill creaks on the prairie.
Bats dipping and rising on ski jumps
are antennae
receiving and transmitting the code.
The whippoorwill interprets the news
from the dead, the unborn.

Exhaustion

The earth is our only bed, the deep
couch from which we cannot fall. Suddenly
this need to lie down.
The flesh will flow out in currents of decay,
a ditch where the weeds find dark treasure.

Toolshed

The sticky smell of rust breaking out in blisters
after every wet spell and burning hoeblades, plows,
crowds the eaves with dryness and wets the lower air.
Dust is stuck to the greased singletree.
Wasp nests like gray sunflowers
hang from tin. The air here hasn't moved
in thirty years, old snow hovering above ground.
Pale weeds grow to cracks.
Half-eaten shovels lean on plows
caked with forty-year-old mud.
Dust drifts crossed by snake zags. Broken clevis.
Plow points are nailed like rusting leaves
to the rafters. Dauber combs dripping plaster.
A bird looks out of its nest in the corner like a dragon
lurking. 1936 license plate,
hames sucked weightless by dry rot.

Cedar

Smell the recorders buried here.
Music lies in the wood
as in the cat's entrails, in ore.
Faint musk of old arrows, canoe ribs.
Wood still giving
its breath, radioactive—releasing
a subtle verb for years
to fill whatever room or closet it lies in
till it's dark, inert
as the wood of cathedral carvings.
Weather leaches the glow
and withes of cool air plunder the fibers. The heat
is drunk off.
The wood reveals in lessening quanta the spice
from a country no one has seen,
leaking from a broken limb expanding to nonexistence.
But inside the scent's strong as light; it repels
the moth as two ends of a magnet
shun meeting.
For they are from the same country, the smell
lunar, musty, an ember so cool
you can hold it in your hand, and the moth
burning out of the dark, its semiquaver
weak as a photograph emerging in the darkroom pan.

Bees Awater

You find one drinking at the creek,
scratching and drinking
before takeoff.
He lifts back
and takes aim, firing homeward.
That's the moment to get your sighting,
get the direction and slant of climb
and you'll be looking right at the tree
on the ridge above
where the honey hangs inside
like cells of a battery
charged with sweetness.
The whole tree has the hum of a transformer.
Bees bubble, circling
like electrons.

Though excited as before a holdup
and hot from the long climb,
you drop the ax
and wait for dark.

LAND DIVING (1976)

Double Springs

I used to wonder how
two springs could issue from the hill
a yard apart. Why not dig deeper
and unite their flow?

And later realized they
surfaced close from opposite
directions. The southern
sweeter, though the northern's steady

effluence came cold, even in the dry
months when its neighbor
slacked and almost stood, with
algae thickening the edges.

In the church nearby I've heard
sermons on the trinity describe
their separate currents merging to
one branch. The sweet uneven

head rose from the hillside leaning toward
Dark Corner, while the constant
icy thread emerged
from the farm country. In summer

they condemned the slow one and
when I came down to drink before
or after preaching its partner sure
enough ran clear, with ebullition

dimpling the surface above the pores,
and purifying lizards gripped
the sandy floor. But after swilling
there I'd dip the gourd

into the slightly silty left
embellished now with leaves and spiders
and aquatic mosses for a richer sip.
That ungodly taste I'd carry home.

Roost Tree

Too wild or many to use the coop
behind his house my uncle's chickens
gathered near sundown close
to an old arborvitae,
still pecking, a few
maybe dusting in the potholes
on the bank.
One by one they'd flap
up into the branches until
the yard was empty and
the waterpans full
of evening sky.
Squawking over favorite
perches and jarring
limbs they shifted like
berries of an abacus on the tiers
of hierarchy,
rooster high in the steeple.
They loaded that old tree
of life miserably,
thirty or forty
whitewashing the trunk
and lower limbs, dripping
even on each other.
The bark they polished
dusty with mites, leafage threadbare.

They settle into dusk clucking;
one flutters down for a last
blade or worm and then back—
disturbing neighbors to
reassert preference.
Frightened by a dog or
possum in the night they
raise a half-hour fuss.
The rooster crows by three.
Sometimes a hen gets heated in her

dream and lets an egg
go, bursting on the limbs
or ground like too-ripe fruit.
The fox may lick its
splatter,
but cannot climb.

Face

The story went that once someone, an unbeliever,
looking into the clouds saw among the luminous
caravan of shapes and smokes, the usual sheep

and outcroppings of battlevapor, signals, choo-
choos, stretching fish, when suddenly in
one great chunk of the sky the Lamb himself,

the face of longhaired Jesus, looked sadly down
at him. Struck down on his way from that moment
he believed. Having a camera he snapped the

quickly dissolving icon. Advertised on radio
and at revivals that photo sold thousands. Looking
at the black and white you never found the image

at first, but when it came rushing out of the
wisps and puffs hardening into a perfect likeness
the recognition was beyond all expectation chilling.

For months I kept eyes ahead or to the ground out
of horror, feared looking back I would see
the Tiger clawing through eastern azure.

Pumpkin

By fall the vines have crawled out
twenty yards from the hill
coiling under weeds.
The great cloth leaves have shriveled
and fallen. No sign of a harvest.
No way to tell where the pumpkins are scattered
except wade into the briars and matted grass,
among hornet nests and snakes,
parting the brush
with a hoe. Or wait
a few weeks longer till the weeds dry
up, burned by frost,
and huge beacons
shine through
like planets submerged and rising.

Compass

One direction, one line of reference,
is all you need to start from
to go anywhere.
And though we don't
the blue sliver
hears
and responds,
aligning with its desire,
to a wind more subtle
than motion. Nervous,
alert,
always remembering
to point home,
a clock with one instant.
Though unsteady as mercury
and constant
only in approximation,
it lays off the horizon, protracting
the possible.

Land Diving

Though it's no disgrace refusing
some things must be done.
And present accomplishment
is no guarantee
of future.
You must come close
as possible without touching
to prove brinkmanship, fly
from the sapling girdered tower
before the whole village, leaping with a scream
against the wall of fear, step onto
the white-hot floor
of emptiness
holding only to yourself.
You will know the pure isolation of fall.
The vines bound to your feet must not snag
on the scaffolding
or they will swing you crushing
into the frame and braces.
They must not break
or be an inch too long
or you will be smothered by
the swat of earth.
Yet the meaning is the closeness.
No stretching out your arms;
you must be jerked to a stop face against
the trampled dirt
by the carefully measured
bonds.
Only they can save you.

Paradise's Fool

In the appletree abloom at the field's
edge and the hummingbird's
nest of moss and plantdown,

in the canticles of the star maiden
and subtle
aesthetics of failure,

the severalty of tidelands, duff
of fencerows, word amulets, stench of traffic
in the electron, I

am paradise's fool.
See the grapery and mariculture, whole
alloys of people, singing plants,

nut groves and
the clitoris sharp as a phonograph needle
scoring circles of music.

Lo, worlds without beginning in
the spring's contact lens,
the haunted well and camphorwood.

Neither in surview nor sweet veld
do I escape the terror,
the presence of the comforter.

TRUNK & THICKET (1978)

Mockingbird

While the bee sleeps in the southern night
and weeds weigh under dowries of dew,
above the distant honky-tonk of falls in
the July dark, before the katydids, when
the only frost is lunar, a voice that
raises the hackles on mountains and chills
the barometric spine, that radios through
many channels in the crab orchard and from
maples above the road. What madrigalist
watering the night with polyphony.
You could see orchestras and oratorios
in the polyglot dark, not so much a
mocking of the many-voiced populations
as a gathering to unlikely congregation
of all song, an anthology including
rooster and cricket broadcast from an ounce
of hot flesh through its briar tongue and filling
the hollows and thickets and dry ditches of
the river valley, soaking under eaves
to the inner ear's accelerator,
circling quick into sleep and bombarding
the ledges of dream.
                                  It is my time then;
I surface like the drowned man after three
days and lie trembling with attention to
the heart's perpetual bass. The dark belongs
to me, the peak of alert night. Mama said,
Then is the time to think about God and
feel close to him. But I float in a
sentient medium that amplifies the
distant creek rubbing its rocks, and mist
muddying the weeds by the dusty road,
and I hear the big distance between stars
where two almost light in the oak by the
window. The ascending particle
contraltos. The river's a great liquid
bird singing all day between boulders,
over logs and around bushy islands.
Empties through the gorge its burden without

lessening. All night sings under hemlocks westering
on the ridges and deep under
stars, loudest in the dark before day.
                    And then—
the house barks and pops in far corners
under eaves. The loudest reports are from
dark tin shrinking. Between come squeaks of a
nail growling from its sheath as a corner
settles. And one hard oakboard jams into
a soft piece of pine giving with sharp jolts
and tremors like microseismic quakes of
plates slipping along a scarp. In damp
weather the distant waterfall sounds close,
brought right to the ear and whispered by
droplets passing the voice on like ions
charging a medium. As if space were a
superconductor heightening all sounds
in a great vowel shift. Night gathers round
its earphones piercing windows in the curtains
as you hear the wail of galaxies and thresh of dust
in canyons of gases, hear the dark
giving birth to stars. Impacts, pings and thuds
from meteorites, splashdown of photons.
Like the music inside a crystal slowly
eaten away. Novas strike and go out.
Sills and cells long forgotten knock and tickle,
tick like boxes hiding their alarms. Even
the genes send out signals, far screams.
Now then, the weed's pharmacy is damp
and busy along the driplines as a typist's
hammers. The nightingale arias steep
as the terrain and various as the
Geographic. As the hen hatches with
her blotting shadow, so ignorance
reveals. Believe in the immaculate
conception of matter from energy.
Wind yodels in the high crevices where
vacuums and near-vacuums vowel its flow.
The dark's a treasure and the mighty skull
of night hurls planetaria. We malinger

where chaos threads and returns like a
windpath across fields. The sea douches
caves and drains the earth's lung. In the windless
dawn snow stands maybe half an inch high on
the fence wires. We hoard our dirt a few
decades while seconds drive pitons of
measure into the jealous mountain. Only
polygraphs reveal time's lie. You will have
the witness of many writings. Coming
up too fast we explode like fish of the
deepest troughs. Stay with high moor and
mountain, the ultraviolet region.
Climb far enough and you reach polar ice
at the equator, get up close to the
bear and dipper. Don't let the mountain's
shadow fall on you like an oilslick, but
as snow on desert canyons, on the
cactus in bloom. Your work will be radical
as the springhead. Start at the beginning
with failure and stand up in the wind. Get
to the bottom and live there, with
land features unaltered by the human.
Work at earthworks, drainages, climates, soils,
find ramparts, embankments, salute agger-making
erosion. Pour footings and drive pilings,
excavate underlying entanglements.
Interpret literally the eros of detail,
the saints of wind and water. Watch the
clearbranch twist and mingle with the trash-filled
creek. Audition for the future. Know time as
magnification, as the sun is
amplified along the horizon. Tend
the rocks as a hen turning her clutch of
eggs. Though drought casehardens soil the night
lets down its milk. See entities beyond
nomination, and let words be vouchers
of time put in among the refuse. Feel the
gully's flowcharts and undertows. Up Hominy
the mountain has been lobotomized. Feel
the church's talon in the night sky.

Collaborate with infusoria
to make new each recumbent giant. What
manitous lurk in the hives of trash
washed up after flood? Making light brings
no illumination. Play with matches,
correspondences. Keep the covenant
with bottomlands and shovel down into
the atom's masonry. Like the banyan
send new trunks to root and spread
into a grove. From the fenlands watch the
mountain's gargoyles. You have spoken.
Now then the accent varies, and from
the flats along the creek in still loftier
cleft that mirrors hawk and partridge. Don't try
to filibuster nature. The art of culture
is always substitution. The knife must
turn to keep its honey. Note nature's
formality and the million intersections
in a piece of cloth. Slice the terrain in
strips evading fungus and depletion, and
play them like bands of the spectrum.
Recombination captures more of sunlight
and mineral. People on mountaintops
age slower, says Einstein. The clock's heart
knocks in its cabinet. Think of vegetal
glass and optical flesh. Though time's a
potentate and clay a tyrant, the law
of conservation means the world's
an anagram of each stage of evolution.
Come red shift in stellar wind, flow sweet as
the milk of new corn.

And the bird outside parodically
now mocking the encyclic dream. The
mountains will not give way and flood us with
the emptiness they hold back all the way to
stars. The sky will maintain its arched
integrity like a hogan roof. Matter
will not burst out of itself without
provocation, critical accumulation.

The dam will not fail with fatigue but feed
evenly through its spillway. History
inpounded above the settlements is stable.
Failure's a kind of dam holding back while
we work the bedrock, fool around in the
valley before shooting the rapids. The
orison high as thermometer's blood.
August the creek goes rabid and froths at
the slightest ripple, builds a head on the
backwater whipping a tough meringue
below the falls going out an eye
at a time. Drools through sticks at the foot
of the pool. The suds wither gummy,
a skim the minnows suck at.

And now from the steep lawn of the pasture
hill a chant more light than voice, many-tongued,
rising through miles of rock and soil. See
lifting deep in the strata to newplowed fields
and under rivers the faraway beginning
of your own resurrection, a heat
moving toward its source. Somewhere your fall
and its rising will coincide as a
missile intercepted by its shadow. Now
it already pursues in a future-seeking
trajectory and whether you turn aside
or run it rises there below the surface
coming steadily on toward the point
of contact and cannot be shaken. As
the reflection of a skydiver thrown
on a far hill rushes to meet its source
at impact, it draws you to its flash.
Every hour contains ice ages, every
second all of evolution. A
single bee whines in the glass hive of the
electric meter where a turntable
plays its recording of power, where the
watt and kilowatt accumulate like
cells of honey. Here multiple wires
feed the clear nipple. The ticker comes in

unseen but counted as the calories of the lake
falling out of itself tally and the
hidden current turrets and the bubble
inflates with electrons. The house
drinks from its tipped jar. Now through
repeating cycles the species stands idling
for a few yugas when out of some distant
nothing a particle, weightless and
chargeless, scores on the chromosome gearbox
shuffling and reengaging the serrated
coins. Without helmsman the thing careers
away onto rocks, over gullies, cliffs,
frottaging trees into the mire, or like a
tortoise stays flipped on its back until
unfueled. Maybe one out of a million
finds a negotiable course, arrives to slip
out of gear again and then idle for
ages in a congenial spot on
higher more defensible ground.
Now then who sings from deep under, beneath
subfloor, sill, and cellar, below foundations,
an artesian voice issuing out of the
crevices to its own stellar level,
slipping from branch to frond in the kelp
forest where bellropes and long tongues
stir to the slightest current, each leaf
containing more chlorophyll than
sequoias, big and sleepy as dinosaurs.
The biggest deserts on the earth lie
underneath. There currents from the poles
howl down the slopes onto the abyssal plain
and roll through canyons never still. Above
fish blow against the ledges like leaves and
butterflies in thermals, flash away like
seeds from maples. And always on the slopes the
planktonic snow settles quietly and loads
the walls until they fail in cloudy slides
that fill the valleys with dust blizzards for
weeks and tear the buried cables. Boulders
rafted from the arctic in ice bomb the

trenches and freezing rivers scour tracks of
stilted swimmers, tripod fish, and plowmarks
of giant worms. In mineral gardens the
charged sea plates rocky nodules slowly.
Bushel snails skim ooze like cream.
Gullies empty silt aprons in bins where tides
winnow the trash of continents. Far up in
the mountains a sandfall carves icy time
where once a meadow heaved its wet grass at
the moon.

I will be what I will be. It is the
dead speaking now from every petal
of the compass, every atom in
the dark traffic. The voice ascends at the
wavelength of mountains out of swamp musk
into the crypt of sky, builds loglog concision
in the night of Babylonian weight,
a table whose bulbed legs whirl gyroscopically
vertical, with grain distinct as the
thumbprint of a file or the ingots of
a snake's belly. Say the statute of
limitations has run out on original
sin, take quiddity of tumbleweed, the
medicine river, take fernbrakes and a
mouse gnawing the atlantic cable to
swill electrons, take rawhide and Cherokees,
the county seat and demonology,
take the stream going underground in late
summer leaving puddles of fry thickening
among white rocks. Take the hotair
balloon lifted by the tongue's candle, take
the sermon as firedrill, take hold of
badlands and dismantle the earth's spinning
integrity for an exploded view. It's
difficult to leave the country where your
ancestors are buried. Take colander
and breeding pond, a sapling with its wrists
cut. Climbing down the tree of Porphyry,
getting it right most when switching and

vacillating. Going east to arrive
west. Walk backwards in the snow leaving
tracks that arrive where they originate
and leave where they are going. Parabolic
sayings augment the ministry of rushes.
Through hatred eat the hidden manna. Let
disinclinations affirm, improvise
a testament, masseur of mud. Seated
wherever speak ex cathedra. Be a
pallbearer of seed into dirt and bear
with solemnity and care the husk of
the ideal to its grave. Shatter the
perfect orbits of atoms to refind
the light buried there. Where is the man who
would not kill to be reborn? I have heard
the pain of the mountain dulcimer
across the cove. Follow the smallest stream
to its cliffs and cross over to the knob
country and the defile to the west, stand
in the electrolytic dark and feel
the creek lick over rocks. Even though you
turn back and circumnavigate do not
turn back. Do not be struck with stagefright on
the summit. Know the buck holds his head
erect when he runs and the doe waves.
Licensed to plead for yourself in
history bear to citydump and fertilizer
plant the thermal waste and bilge of learning.
Dive beneath the thermocline and come up
like a pale sprout from the darkroom.
Unable to find a parking place in
the city don't panic. You are one gene
in the cells of the body of language.
Go fast awake through the laurel slicks, the
electric blanket of foliage. Since
nobody understands more than a fraction
at a time it's good to keep records. Don't
confidence theory. Carry these sayings
to the south breeze, to the dirt's craw, the
ground spewed up with frost. Create brief

Yoknapatawphas, a potlatch of words.
Climb through the thickets of Big Hungry
AWOL from society. Take bat's milk, the
eagle's seed, and sleep in coral underbrush.
Each rock and bit of trash is an avatar
and mud hardening to crust a voice.
The virtual coil of dust is erotic.
Thirsty ventricles gulp and swallow.
Mountains speak in tongues. Take the wide thought
of estuaries. The absent god leaves the forest
and tundra soaked in divinity. In
Egyptian silence, trappist restraint, hear
thunder. Being is fed by time as by
oxygen. Swampwater's black as a new
cadillac. Take Saluda River and
Shoestring Creek and Bullpen Gap. Don't cringe at
the thought of Grandma with her birch toothbrush
and the sullen sentiment of isolated
coves. Take the timbered-off slopes and the
stumphouse on Eyelet Ridge. Build with undressed
stone. An illiterate ancestor won the
battle of Cowpens. Reject the dryhides and
take the holy dance. Take the land beyond
the fall-line, beyond the corduroy road
and depot, and ford the creek lengthwise to
get into town. Offer reticence and disapprobation,
follow no trade, and heading for deep cover
come to an opening in the canopy
where light shines from obscure places. Hide
behind a waterfall in congregation
with mist and rock. Take the justified
margin of cornfields. Inaugurate by
leaving, ordained by anonymity.

GROUNDWORK (1979)

Mountain Bride

They say Revis found a flatrock
on the ridge just
perfect for a natural hearth,
and built his cabin with a stick

and clay chimney right over it.
On their wedding night he lit
the fireplace to dry away the mountain
chill of late spring and flung on

applewood to dye
the room with molten color while
he and Martha that was a Parrish
warmed the sheets between the tick

stuffed with leaves and its feather
cover. Under that wide hearth
a nest of rattlers,
they'll knot a hundred together,

had wintered and were coming awake.
The warming rock
flushed them out early.
It was she

who wakened to their singing near
the embers and roused him to go look.
Before he reached the fire
more than a dozen struck

and he died yelling her to stay
on the big four-poster.
Her uncle coming up the hollow
with a gift bearham two days later

found her shivering there
marooned above a pool
of hungry snakes,
and the body beginning to swell.

Death Crown

In the old days back when
one especially worthy lay dying
for months, they
say the feathers in the pillow would
knit themselves into a crown
that those attending felt in perfect
fit around the honored head.
The feather band they took to be
certain sign of another crown,
the saints and elders of the church,
the Deep Water Baptists said.
I've seen one unwrapped from its
cloth in the attic, the down
woven perfect and tight for
over a century, shiny but
soft and light almost as light.

Canning Time

The floor was muddy with the juice of peaches
and my mother's thumb, bandaged for the slicing,
watersobbed. She and Aunt Wessie skinned
bushels that day, fat Georgia Belles
slit streaming into the pot. Their knives
paid out limp bands onto the heap
of parings. It took care to pack the jars,
reaching in to stack the halves
firm without bruising, and lowering
the heavy rack into the boiler already
trembling with steam, the stove malignant
in heat. As Wessie wiped her face
the kitchen sweated its sweet filth.
In that hell they sealed the quickly browning
flesh in capsules of honey, making crystals
of separate air across the vacuums.
The heat and pressure were enough to grow
diamonds as they measured hot
syrup into quarts. By supper the last jar
was set on the counter to cool
into isolation. Later in the night
each little urn would pop as it
achieved its private atmosphere and
we cooled into sleep, the stove now
neutral. The stones already
pecked clean in the yard were free to try
again for the sun. The orchard meat fixed in
cells would be taken down cellar in the
morning to stay gold like specimens
set out and labeled, a vegetal
battery we'd hook up later. The women
too tired to rest easily think of
the treasure they've laid up today
for preservation at coffin level, down there
where moth and rust and worms corrupt,
a first foundation of shells to be
fired at the winter's muddy back.

Bean Money

Back from the market late with a watermelon
and his bib-pocket full of cash
my father shoved a fist of back-pay
for the summer at me, the yield from
digging holes and tying strings,
lugging hampers in the rain with heat rash,
stings and blisters. In my room I'd sit
with dirty feet and sweat-ripe skin
on the sheets and unwad the damp bills
to press in stacks like pages of a ledger
of the hot days, the green and gray ink
more lasting than sunburn or calluses,
and telling of my labor with a one-eye
lit pyramid. I collated
and banded the leaves in bundles
and counted out the coins like next year's
seeds into the old tobacco pouch.
That consecrated metal was an abstract
drawn off the soil and sweat and
cast into a jewelry of value.
I meant those struck emblems to act
as compact fuel, like nuclear pellets,
to power my long excursion out of the sun
and beyond the ridges, and put
them all in a paper box above the closet
door to trade later; the young summers
become signs to be translated
again into paper, ink and paper,
in the cool timeless leisure I saw
while washing my feet on the back steps
and spitting melon seeds
into the cricket-haunted dark.

Wallowing

When Old Nell rolled in the bins
hollowed out of the pasture flats, she
whinnied with the pleasure
as one ripened area of skin after
another whetted the firm ground,
shuddered and twisted to reach
itches on withers and rump.
She seemed more like a snake or worm there
on her back, often pulsing in coital
shiver like an amoeba.
I knew she scrubbed of fly eggs,
dung, dried blood from bites,
in the rasp of sand,
the emery submersion salving
harness galls and currying off sweat,
massaging the soreness of age.
Finding still neglected precincts
she'd press them with a snort to
dry grass at the lip of the wallow,
stoking and frisking hair roots,
and getting down into the trough
generate with friction a field of brushed
nerves. She indulged a third of her
hide at once to the bump and tickle,
running with the pasture on her back.
She thrashed the late summer dust
in a whirlpool, then
stood and shook herself of the dry
cloud and, smoking pure and free
as if new-born in the depression,
stepped onto the wide pasture.

Bricking the Church

At the foot of Meetinghouse Hill
where once the white chapel
pointed among junipers and pulled
a wash of gravestones west,

they've buried the wooden snow that
answered sarvis in bloom
and early morning fogs, in brick,
a crust the same dull red

as clay in nearby gullies.
The little churchhouse now looks more
like a post office or school.
It's hard to find

among the brown winter slopes
or plowed fields of spring.
Brick was prestigious back when
they set their minds and savings to it.

They wanted to assert its form
and presence if not in stone
at least in hardened earth, urban weight,
as the white clapboards replaced

unpainted lumber which replaced
the logs of the original
where men brought their guns to preaching
and wolves answered the preacher.

The structure grows successive rings,
and as its doctrine softens
puts on a hard shell
for weathering this world.

Burning the Hornet's Nest

The great paper lantern in the appletree
does not come on at dark, is shaded
even from starlight. But waiting
until night you climb up into the belfry

of limbs and feel it near,
approach not jarring the branch
it's soldered to. A rancid
heat emanates from where

they sleep, a crackling like acid working.
Light the kerosene-soaked cob and jab
at the aperture. Burning, the fabric
eyeball seems even bigger. Jerking

outer layers catch and peel
upwards. Pellets drip out.
The sunflower heads of wet
larvae are reluctant, seethe

like juices and drop off whole post offices
of trout bait smoldering in the damp
weeds. Next morning survivors clamp
to the rags hanging around the empty socket.

Zircon Pit

Just below the crest of Meetinghouse Hill
I used to climb the apron of spoil
into a digging long abandoned. Leaves
and saplings hid the raw dirt and the hole,
half-filled in fall, fit like a nest
from which to drowse and look
down the steepness and keep watch
on my century. One of the high places.
I spent hours there in late winter,
warmed by leaves and the solartrap, just
out of the summit winds compressing
across the rim. Caught the best sun, the new light
of February when the mountains
pressed clean by snow began to twitch
and trickle. From that blind
I watched the mailman on the creekroad
hours before he reached our box.
The only gem found where Great-Grandpa dug
was the many-facet thrill and vantage of remoteness.
Sometimes the whole forest seemed to river
up and over my lookout and burn
vivid, then drain into the present.
I listened, close to the new sky.

Secret Pleasures

The sourwood sprouts are long
as flyrods in the field we turned-out
years ago. Its soil had worn
so thin the weeds runted and rocks,
boiled up by frost, began to cobble-over
bare spots and gather in the washes.
Erosion left the ground in swells like graves.
Our granary's now the weathered humps
of clay from which we took
the syrup and left
a fragrant dust. Let it
scab and fur over on its own
and offer no crop bigger than dew
and the beadwork of berrypicking.
My secret pleasure: to come and watch
these shoots work up
their honey from bitter clay.
Lichen gardens improve the scars,
patching over history. I offer
the land my leisure.

AT THE EDGE OF THE ORCHARD COUNTRY
(1987)

Passenger Pigeons

Remembering the descriptions by Wilson
and Bartram, and Audubon and other
early travelers to the interior, of the sky
clouded with the movements of winged pilgrims
wide as the Mississippi, wide as the Gulf
Stream, hundred-mile epics of equidistant wings
horizon to horizon, how their droppings
splashed the lakes and rivers, how
where they roosted whole forests broke down
worse than from ice storms, and the woods floor
was paved with their lime, how the settlers
got them with ax and gun and broom
for hogs, how when a hawk attacked
the endless stream bulged away
and kept the shift long after
the raptor was gone, and having read how
the skies of America became silent, the fletched
oceans forgotten, how can I replace
the hosts of the sky, the warm-blooded jetstreams?
To echo the birdstorms of those early
sunsets, what high river of electron, cell and star?

Horace Kephart

Outside the tent on the Little Fork
of the Sugar Fork of Hazel Creek
a man is writing. His table boards
on upended kegs, he drafts meticulously clear
paragraphs and weights the finished pages
with a shotgun shell. Squirrels rippling
in the trees above do not distract him.
The jug by a white pine is stopped with a cob.

Each sentence he scratches with economy
is payment on a vast unpayable obligation:
to his parents for the years of college, for
the special courses at Cornell, for his tenure
cataloguing Petrarch in Florence, for the girl,
his Laura, married in Ithaca and taken
west, for the librarian's post in St. Louis,
for the study of Finnish, for the unwritten
history of western exploration that
excused long camping holidays and nights
away from home and expensive rare editions,
for the weeks of drinking and sulk.

Lean as a mountaineer himself, galluses
swung at his sides, he scribbles to the young
his intensity of woodcraft, weapons, survival,
and of the hillmen his archaic friends and landlords,
makers of spirits. Even now one's loose
hog crashes through the brush into his camp
and knocks a tentline from its stob so
the canvas home sags at one corner on
his narrow cot, and breaks the clothesline.
As he jumps to shout and whack it back
into the undergrowth the unfinished sheet
from an early chapter of *Our Southern Highlanders*
peels off the desk and luffs like a wounded
dove out through the scrub and leaves to the creek.

Buffalo Trace

Sometimes in the winter mountains
after a little snow has blown in the night
and nothing's alive in eye-range
but the clouds
near peaks frozen clean
in the solstice sun,
the white finds a faint depression
to stick in out of wind
and makes visible for the first time
through woods and along the slopes
to where it nicks the rim
perceptibly, a ghostpath
under brush and broomsedge,
merging in the pasture with narrow
cowtrails but running on through fences
and across boundaries, under branches
in tattered sweep out to the low
gaps of the old migrations
where they browsed into the summer mountains
then ebbed back into the horizon
and back of the stars.

White Autumn

She had always loved to read, even
in childhood during the Confederate War,
and built the habit later of staying up
by the oil lamp near the fireplace after
husband and children slept, the scrub-work done.
She fed the addiction in the hard years
of Reconstruction and even after
her husband died and she was forced
to provide and be sole foreman of the place.
While her only son fought in France
it was this second life, by the open window
in warm months when the pines on the hill
seemed to talk to the creek, or katydids
lined-out their hymns in the trees beyond the barn,
or by the familiar of fire in winter,
that sustained her. She and her daughters
later forgot the time, the exact date,
if there was such a day, she made her decision.
But after the children could cook
and garden and milk and bring in a little
by housecleaning for the rich in Flat Rock,
and the son returned from overseas
wounded but still able and married a war widow,
and when she had found just the right chair,
a rocker joined by a man over on Willow
from rubbed hickory, with cane seat and back,
and arms wide enough to rest her everlasting cup
of coffee on, or a heavy book,
she knew she had come to her place and would stay.
And from that day, if it was one time and not
a gradual recognition, she never crossed a threshold
or ventured from that special seat of rightness,
of presence and pleasure, except to be helped to bed
in the hours before dawn for a little nap.
That chair—every Christmas someone gave her a bright
cushion to break in—was the site on which she bathed
in a warm river of books and black coffee,
varieties of candy and cakes kept in a low cupboard
at hand. The cats passed through her lap and legs

and through the rungs of her seat. The tons
of firewood came in cold and left as light, smoke, ash.
She rode that upright cradle to sleep
and through many long visits with tiers of family,
kissing the babies like different kinds of fruit.
Always hiding the clay pipe in her cabinet
when company appeared. She chaired decisions
to keep the land and refused welfare.
On that creaking throne she ruled a tiny kingdom
through war, death of kin. Even on the night she did
stop breathing, near a hundred, no one knew
exactly when, but found the lamp still on,
the romance open to a new chapter,
and the sun just appearing at her elbow.

Yellow

May is the yellow month. At this
latitude the woods are a fog of different
yellow-greens as first leaves
open pages and new twigs on the willows
grow bright as chicken fat.
In every yard the daffodils and dandelions,
and clouds of wild mustard light
the open fields, even as wind
bruises cowlicks in the rye. Along
highways and parks forsythia
sprays its heat, and fire rinses seedbeds
of old stalks at dark. The day begins
in a golden antiquity, flushing
the ridges so they echo inside the room
where flesh stretches into flower, where
even the interior of night is saffroned
the most erotic color of touch and know.

Manure Pile

Heaped gold and powerful behind the barn.
The crust, faded by weather, almost
never freezes, steaming off snow with fever
of its inner work. Birds worry
the seeds exposed by rain.
Black chemistry of the core
nurses weeds on the baked hide
while the yard is frost-dead. Once
a little chick peeped from its straw
in January, hatched by the warmth.
The matter dug from its side for fields
is too strong even for worms to live in,
sealed years by the ammonia.
Haunted in the hot months by a genie
of flies, it jewels the downwind.
Sundays the many purple butterflies
that suck its inks, shiver off into the sky
where carillons of convection ring.

Lightning Bug

Carat of the first radiance,
you navigate like a creature
of the deep. I wish I could read
your morse across the night yard.
Your body is a piece of star
but your head is obscure. What small
photography! What instrument
panel is on? You are winnowed
through the hanging gardens of night.
Your noctilucent syllables
sing in the millennium of
the southern night with star-talking
dew, like the thinker sending nous
into the outerstillness from
the edge of the orchard country.

Radio

In the corner farthest from the fire,
a safe of carved oak,
cabinet of voices.
The gothic windows stretched with cloth
hide a powerful hum when Grandpa
rolls the knob and the numbers
light up as the needle
passes in its window.
He hunts for the combination.
Birds back somewhere among
the preachers, static, whine
and whistle late at night from forests.
I want to reach in there
and find the jars that sing,
and watch through a gap in the back
the vials glowing in the muck of wires,
a throbbing in the metal
where the languages of the air
are trapped and spoken.
That space unreachable in the small light,
poisoned by electricity.

The Gift of Tongues

The whole church got hot and vivid
with the rush of unhuman chatter
above the congregation,
and I saw my father looking at
the altar as though electrocuted.
It was a voice I'd never heard
but knew as from other centuries.
It was the voice of awful fire.
"What's he saying?" Ronald hissed
and jabbed my arm. "Probably Hebrew."
The preacher called out another
hymn, and the glissade came again,
high syllables not from my father's
lips but elsewhere, the flare of
higher language, sentences of light.
And we sang and sang again, but
no one rose as if from sleep to
be interpreter, explain the writing
on the air that still shone there like
blindness. None volunteered a gloss
or translation or receiver
of the message. My hands hurt
when pulled from the pew's varnish
they'd gripped and sweated so. Later,
standing under the high and plain-
sung pines on the mountain, I clenched
my jaws like pliers, holding in
and savoring the gift of silence.

Bellrope

The line through the hole in the dank
vestibule ceiling ended in
a powerful knot worn slick, swinging
in the breeze from those passing. Half
an hour before service Uncle
Allen pulled the call to worship,
hauling down the rope like the starting
cord of a motor, and the tower
answered and answered, fading
as the clapper lolled aside. I watched
him before Sunday school heave on
the line as on a wellrope. And
the wheel creaked up there as heavy
buckets emptied out their startle
and spread a cold splash to farthest
coves and hollows, then sucked the rope
back into the loft, leaving just
the knot within reach, trembling
with its high connections.

Uncle Robert

M/Sgt. Robert G. Levi 1915–1943
Serial No. 34119284
813th Bomb Sqdn.
482nd Bombardment Group
Eighth Air Force

In the little opening in the woods
your cot springs were a crisp red wool
on the moss. While we raked leaves
for the cowstall Grandma told me how
you came up here on summer afternoons
to read and paint and sleep after
working the hootowl shift at the cottonmill.
You must have meant to return to leave
your couch on the innerspring moss
on the mountainside.

        The metalwork you did
in the CCC—toolbox, a vase, buckets
thick as stoves—was scattered through the house
and barn. I lost your flies and tackle
in the weeds above the garden, and stuck
your chevron patches to my flannel shirt.
In the messkit returned from England
I fried sand like snow, and found
the picture of your fiancée in the cedarchest.

It was hinted I was "marked" somehow,
not only by your name, but in some way
unexplained was actually you. Aunts and cousins
claimed we favored and I spoke with your stammer.
Your paintings watched me
from the bedroom wall and mantel
and your poem clipped from the paper
yellowed among the rationbooks. I inherited
your Testament with its boards of carved cedar,

and the box of arrowheads you picked
from the dust of bottomlands on Sunday afternoons
like seeds and teeth of giants.

No one opened the steel coffin sent back
to see what bone splinters or rags
had been found where the B-17 novaed
above East Anglia. I touched the ribbons
and medals in the bureau, the gold buttons.
Your canoe lay in the barnloft for years
between the cornpile and the wall, heavy
with dust as the boat in a pyramid
and tracked by mice and swallows. The paint
and canvas curled away from the cedar slats.
I meant to use it someday but never dared:
it was not creekworthy without new skin
and too heavy for one to carry. I turned
it over and looked into the belly
and sat on the webbed seat, rocking
on the corn-bearinged floor. Once hornets
built in the prow what I imagined
was a skull with honey brains. On snowy days
I sat there and paddled across the wilderness
of loft dark. The summer before you left
you portaged to the river and back,
then carried the canoe up there.
Something was always scary about the craft:
each time I turned it over fearing to see
a body inside. It lay among the shucks
and fodder as though washed up by a flood
and stranded forever.

                One day I found your bugle
in the attic, velveted with dust and lint.
The brass felt damp with corrosion,
the bell dented and dark as leather.
I took it out behind the house and,
facing west, blew into the cold mouthpiece

a hopeful syllable. The metal trembled
and blared like a sick steer, went quiet.
I poured all my body heat into the barrel
and a sour flatulence shook out and echoed
off the mountains. I made half-musical
squeaks and bursts till dizzy, aiming vowels
like watermelon seeds into the tube.
When the groans returned from Buzzard Rock
I thought they must be wails from the cove
for someone dead, and nothing I had sent,
or the ghost of a train lost in the valley
and relayed like an aural mirage from
the past still with us and talking back.

The flag that draped your casket was kept
folded in the trunk. They said
I had the high-arched "Levi foot"
like you, and your quick laugh. I was told
you made your own marbles as a boy
by rolling branch clay into balls and baking
in the oven. Mama liked to take out
of cloth a clay statue of a naked man
face down in the dirt which you once
modeled and called "The Dying Warrior."
I marveled at the cunning work of leg
and tiny arms and spilling hair, and touched
your fingerprints still clear on the base.

Chant Royal

Born in a notch of the high mountains where
a spring ran from under the porch, on
the second of April just one hundred years
ago this month, my grandpa was a weak one
to start with, premature, weighed a scant
two pounds twelve ounces. So fragile the aunt
who tended that first night feared to move
him except for feeding and the placing of
diapers. He slept near the fire in a shoebox
with one end cut out. Against the odds he would prove
adequate for survival, withstanding all knocks.

Because he was puny his mother would rear
him sheltered, keep him beside her out of the sun
and rain alike, feed him molasses and sulfur in fear
of worms and would let him walk, not run,
to the gap with the others to stand on the slant
bars while the cows were milked in elegant
twilight. Pious and hard, she showed her love
through strictness and was known to reprove
him for the least resistance. She tried raw
grape juice and teas of the yarb grannies, strove,
adequate for survival, withstanding all knocks,

to find faith healers, quacks, to cure
her youngest. A cousin wrote of Dr. Wilson
down near Greenville. They took the wagon one clear
morning and reached the town just as the moon
rose full. The man at the door said, "I can't
see you this late," but examined and began to rant
on the virtues of tobacco ("Give him a chew"), then shove
and shoo them out. That night they drove
all the way back. No telling what unlocks
vitality: from that day he began to grow and rove
adequate for survival, withstanding all knocks.

Frampold as any mountain branch, he hunted bees and deer,
carried to mill on Cold Friday and learned the fun
of shivarees and drinking. Saw his father appear

walking through the pasture toward him and beckon,
then vanish when he spoke like any haint,
and die within the month. He heard a panther
scream and follow as he came back through the cove
from hogkilling, and sat up nights by the stove
while his brother crisised with the fever and tried to mock
death before it cooled him. Nobody who saw the dove
was adequate for survival, withstanding all knocks.

Out sanghunting he met Mrs. Capps and her
daughter sawing crosscut. The girl could stun
with her beauty, hiding bare feet under leaves. Inner
currents stirred. He quit drinking, came to church, and won
her after three weeks' courting. But they lived in want
the first year; a child died. He made his covenant
one cold night in the orchard and a trove
came in acres for sale cheap on the creek above
the Andrews place. There he sank a well through rock,
weathered debt, depression, set groves,
adequate for survival, withstanding all knocks.

Envoi

Guardian ghost, inhere herein. Before Jove
may this music honor his example, improve
my time as he invested his, and no less unorthodox
discover significance in the bonds his fate wove
adequate for survival, withstanding all knocks.

Firecrackers at Christmas

In the Southern mountains, our big
serenade was not the Fourth but
always Christmas Eve and Christmas.
Starting at midnight the valleys
and branch coves fairly shook with barks
of crackers, boom of shotguns, jolt
even of sticks of dynamite.
You would have thought a new hunting
season had begun in the big-star
night, or that a war had broken
out in the scattered hollows: all
the feuds and land disputes come to
a magnum finale. The sparks
everywhere of match and fuse
and burst were like giant lightning bugs.
Thunder doomed the ridges though
the sky shone clear and frost sugared
the meadows. Yankees were astonished
at the violence and racket
on the sacred day, they said, as
cherrybombs were hurled into yards
and placed expanding mailboxes
same as Halloween. Perhaps the custom
had its origins in peasant-pagan
times of honoring the solstice
around a burning tree, or in
the mystery centuries of
saluting the miraculous
with loudest brag and syllable.
Certainly the pioneer had
no more valuable gift to bring
than lead and powder to offer
in the hush of hills, the long rifles
their best tongues for saying the peace
they claimed to carry to the still
unchapeled wilderness, just as
cannon had been lit in the Old
World to announce the birth of kings.
They fired into the virgin skies

a ceremony we repeated
ignorantly. But what delight
I felt listening in the unheated
bedroom dark, not believing in
Santa Claus or expensive gifts,
to the terrible cracks along
the creek road and up on Olivet,
as though great rivers of ice were
breaking on the horizon and
trees were bursting at the heart
and new elements were being born
in whip-stings and distant booms
and the toy chatter of the littlest
powder grace notes. That was our
roughest and best caroling.

Man and Machine

Besides drinking and telling lies,
nothing interested my cousin Luther
like working with the tractor.
Astride that bright and smelly beast
he was a man inspired.
Revving and tearing the stubble
of early spring he cussed
the metal like a favorite mule,
parrying any stallout with the shift.
In too big a hurry to turn
at the end of a row he jammed
in a brake and spun around,
lowered the harrows
into the winter-bleached field
and blasted off for yon end.
Barely able to read, he took
dusters and bush hogs and diesel movements
apart with the skill of a surgeon,
hollering on the phone for parts
as far away as Charlotte or Atlanta.
Would stay on his ass at the filling station
or country store for weeks
while wife and kids and parents
picked in the heat the crops he'd
drive to market. Neither storm-threat
nor overripening could move him
to join their labor. Until time
for dusting with the homemade blower
mounted on a jeep. Or after the vines
were cut he'd windlass in the long wires.
Winters Luther lived only for his truck,
banging down the dirt road to Chestnut Springs
for booze and women. But that was just
occasional. Most days he'd brag at the store
about his pickup, or be trading for another
with even thicker tires, more horsepower
and chrome, a gunrack in the window.
At home he'd maybe tune a little,
oil the plates of the planter.

But off the machine he was just
another stocky hoojer, yelling
to make up for his lack of size
and self-esteem, adding fat and blood
pressure. Late February breaking time
transformed him. He leapt on the big
diesel and burned out its winter farts
all the way to the bottoms, whipping
the animal until it glowed, became
his legs and voice and shoulders.
To children and himself he tore up ground
like a centaur. Plowing with the lights on
all night in the river fields
he circled more times than any race driver,
shouting in the settling damp while
we slept hearing the distant fury.
And by morning the fields were new.

Field Theory

In those days they grew sweet potatoes
big as newborn babies, and discovered
the power of clouds in boilers.
The spring said its diamonds under the poplars
and the spine twinkled like a milkyway.
Children shouted kickball and tag
from early evening until dark in the pasture.
I like to think they found in work
a soil subliminal and sublime.
Their best conspiracies were two
breathing in the night. They lived
on the upland atoll and didn't care
to step on horizons. And left no more
trace than a cloud shadow when I woke
from the coils of the cell's heart,
in the non-euclidean mountains,
recovering pieces of the morgenland.

SIGODLIN (1990)

Sigodlin

When old carpenters would talk of buildings
out of plumb or out of square, they always
said they were sigodlin, as though anti-
sigodlin meant upright and square, at proper
angles as a structure should be, true to
spirit level, plumb line, erect and sure
from the very center of the earth, firm
and joined solid, orthogonal and right,
no sloping or queasy joints, no slouching
rafters and sills. Those men made as they were:
the heavy joists and studs yoked perfectly,
and showing the dimensions themselves, each
mated pair of timbers to embody
and enact the crossing of space in its
real extensions, the vertical to be
the virtual pith of gravity, horizontal
aligned with the surface of the planet at
it local tangent. And what they fitted
and nailed or mortised into place, downright
and upstanding, straight up and down and flat
as water, established the coordinates
forever of their place in creation's
fabric, in a word learned perhaps from
masons who heard it in masonic rites
drawn from ancient rosicrucians who
had the term from the Greek mysteries'
love of geometry's power to say,
while everything in the real may lean just
the slightest bit sigodlin or oblique,
the power whose center is everywhere.

Audubon's Flute

Audubon in the summer woods
by the afternoon river sips
his flute, his fingers swimming on
the silver as silver notes pour

by the afternoon river, sips
and fills the mosquito-note air
with silver as silver notes pour
two hundred miles from any wall.

And fills the mosquito-note air
as deer and herons pause, listen,
two hundred miles from any wall,
and sunset plays the stops of river.

As deer and herons pause, listen,
the silver pipe sings on his tongue
and sunset plays the stops of river,
his breath modeling a melody

the silver pipe sings on his tongue,
coloring the trees and canebrakes,
his breath modeling a melody
over calamus and brush country,

coloring the trees and canebrakes
to the horizon and beyond,
over calamus and brush country
where the whitest moon is rising

to the horizon and beyond
his flute, his fingers swimming on
where the whitest moon is rising.
Audubon in the summer woods.

Inertia

There is such a languor to matter,
every mass asserting presence
while soaring in its stasis.
Electrons spin and molecules
twitch, yet the material resists
all change of direction, defends
its momentum and moment, in
the reverie of substance, the
immobility and dream of
the body's authority of weight,
remaining undisturbed, by poise
of precedence, occupation,
reluctant as a bear to wake
from the immanence and ponder,
the gravity of mere artlessness.

Odometer

We glance always at this little
window of the slowest slot machine
to calendar our progress out.
The meter not ticking is active
just the same, summing up distance
toward the big question, the rollers
marking off ground and still counting.
We're happy no matter how far
gone, to be clocking off the miles,
to keep on breaking our own record
of progress, to make the old wreck
go another revolution
of the thousand wheel, and the ten,
as one candy-size roll of our
numbers turns up another ten times
slower until they all turn up,
in the ode to travel, zero
zero zero zero zero
as it was in the beginning.

Rearview Mirror

This little pool in the air is
not a spring but sink into which
trees and highway, bank and fields are
sipped away to minuteness. All
split on the present then merge in
stretched perspective, radiant in
reverse, the wide world guttering
back to one lit point, as our way
weeps away to the horizon
in this eye where the past flies ahead.

Vietnam War Memorial

What we see first seems a shadow
or a retaining wall in the park,
like half a giant pool or half
an exposed foundation. The names
start a few to the column at
the shallow ends and grow panel
by deeper panel as though month
by month to the point of opposing
planes. From that pit you can't see much
official Washington, just sky
and trees and names and people on
the Mall and the Capitol like
a fancy urn. For this is a wedge
into the earth, a ramp of names
driven into the nation's green,
a black mirror of names many
as the text of a book published
in stone, beginning almost
imperceptibly in the lawn
on one side and growing on black
pages bigger than any reader
(as you look for your own name in
each chapter) and then thin away
like a ledger into turf again,
with no beginning, no end. As though
the black wall uncovered here a few
rods for sunlight and recognition
runs on and on through the ground in
both directions, with all our names
on the hidden panels, while
these names shine in the open noon.

Mountain Graveyard

stone   notes

slate   tales

sacred   cedars

heart   earth

asleep   please

hated   death

Heaven

And yet I don't want not to believe in,
little as I can, the big whoosh of souls
upward at the Rapture, when clay and ocean,
dust and pit, yield up their dead, when all

elements reassemble into the forms
of the living from the eight winds and flung
petals of the compass. And I won't assume,
much as I've known it certain all along,

that I'll never see Grandma again, nor
Uncle Vol with his fabulations,
nor see Uncle Robert plain with no scar
from earth and the bomber explosions.

I don't want to think how empty and cold
the sky is, how distant the family,
but of winged seeds blown from a milkweed field
in the opalescent smokes of early

winter ascending toward heaven's blue,
each self orchestrated in one aria
of river and light. And those behind the blue
are watching even now us on the long way.

Sidney Lanier Dies at Tryon 1881

The chill mountain air grew stingy
with oxygen after the long
carriage ride from Fletcher across
the Ridge and down the Thermal Belt
to the house outside Tryon.
Two months of camping on the peaks
only made the world more hazy,
ghostlike, and the summit winds had
sucked away his breath, and stolen
his voice, the form and duration
of English phrasing he'd worked so
to make measurable, to set down.
And the current pouring from his lips
into the flute had vanished
and only turbulence and coughs
and random winds were left gusting,
subsiding in his head. The blood
seemed at times to want to break
out of his heart and through the skin
of his forehead to taste air, to
quench its awful heat. The blood he
spat and blood humming in his ears
and in the manly condition
only Mary understood made
him think of sunrise, the rose-lit
mornings in army camps, in
the prison pits and mud. The one
oratorio, all notes and language,
seemed red as coals, red as his
syllables, while the night he'd married
hovered near, and his son the shadow,
and the world somewhere gaudy and
subtle as Shakespeare drew further
back, swam on the higher oceans.
The black peaks beyond the house looked
down, and there was a certain phrase,
a ripple, a little turn on
the flute he must try to recall,
that ran the same as the dark ridge

looming at the window yesterday,
and he could almost remember
the precise fingering, the pause
and the continuing line, just
as the world became visible.

Writing Spider

When Uncle Wass had found the spider's
W woven between the limbs
of a dead chestnut over on
the Squirrel Hill, he said he knew
there would be war. But even before
Pearl Harbor he was gone himself
and my Grandpa, his brother, told
how the writing spider's runes could spell
a message to the world, or warn
of the individual reader's own
end with an initial. That web
was strung significant as lines
in a palm and the little webster,
spinning out its monogram like
the fates, put the whole dictionary
of a life in one elaborate
letter to be abstracted from
the Jacob's ladder of floss and dew
in the eye of the beholder,
a lifetime's work for it and all.

The Body of Elisha Mitchell

The body of Elisha Mitchell
when it lay in the clear pool
beneath a waterfall below
his named and measured peak, white as
marble in the laurel gloom, was
stirred by shock ripples from the falls
and turned by eddies like a compass
needle pointing to the summit.
The icy spring water had kept
the body perfect for two weeks
as the searchers crisscrossed the Blacks,
Big Tom Wilson the bear hunter
and the Reverend Mitchell Junior
hacking into thickets to look
at every twig for sign of tracks.
They came to a cliff edge and saw
the body fifty feet below
staring past them at the peak
he'd measured highest in the east,
his eyes wide and blue and clear
as the eye of his barometer
used to get elevation. The
snowy body was unbruised by
rock or tree in the plunge, untouched
by fish or animal, though prick
marks would hint a rattler strike
may have sent him reeling down
the slope and over, falling numb,
the venom perfect for embalming,
the body white as a breathless statue.

Shaking

For us a handshake was a duel:
two boys in a friendly clasp
of greeting were fighting the test
of power. Who squeezed first might have
an advantage, unless the cold
tendons got strained, and the grip,
so big and cruel at once would
weaken from the quick exertion
as the other built up a grasp
that overrode and then melted
the opposing hand, while we both
kept grinning hello. But the best
defense was to cup your palm so
knuckles weren't aligned for grinding
but curled under the hostile force.
It was the feint of giving in,
while the rival bore down and thought
himself near victory that was
the last strategy. And when he
crunched you toward acquiescence and
withdrawal from the lethal shake,
you put everything, your whole weight
and blood and warmth and thought, pumped down
through shoulder and elbow and wrist
on the opponent's paw as his
smile registered surprise and pain
and you broke down his control in
the vise of your own gesture of
reciprocation, serious welcome.

The Way Back

Having wound and banged himself down
into the sewers of the mountain, crawled
through eyes in the rock and fallen
where the silted floor is slick as an intestine,
the string dropped or broken way back,
he quarrels with his echoes and tests his will
by climbing, feet and fingers, to fall
sickened by the slap of cheek on mud.
He tries every niche and alcove and side tunnel,
swings around stalactites and stirs
bats like forgotten sins while standing
in their lice-flanneled dung, and meets
the beast of his fear, the shaggy king
of griefs, and whipped by anger in the shivery dark,
strangles him. He sits now against the bedrock
swallowing the dead air and listening
beyond the obscure drip for voice or footstep.
Only the hurry of breath and heartbeat, his.
His eyes strain at the dark for the faintest
difference. No ghost in the smothering air.
He sweats in filth at the final wall,
warpainted with his blood. Amazed.
So this is what it means to die a hero,
far from the breeze of day, from the known
and loved? He would not have thought it could end
unseen. But a hair is stuck to the gore on his hand.
The single thread runs out and he pulls to see
if it holds. In the struggle he had not felt it.
The sweet thread runs out into the dark
tight as though unbroken. Feeling with his feet,
hoping he won't stumble and drop the line,
he handwalks it grasp by grasp tasting the sweetness
between thumb and shaking finger, working along
too joyed almost to breathe around corners
and across the now-familiar pools, back toward
the mouth and daylight with its clouds
there above the ridge, to her with the tall forehead
who gave him this fine clue so long ago.

When He Spoke Out of the Dark

When he spoke out of the dark I
had not seen him sitting there in
a lawn chair on the grass resting
in his white painter's overalls
and gray sweatshirt and cap, gray hands,
easing after the long workday.
For the milking was over, and
weeds pulled for the hog, kindling had
been cut and the painting done,
the masonry and carpentry,
the holes had been dug, the corn hoed,
beans carried out of mud, the ditch
opened, the corn gathered and heaved
into the barn loft and shelled and
carried to mill. And there he sat,
tired, where I had not seen him,
looming to my dark-adjusting eyes
white and smokelike out of the depths
of night, and spoke close as anyone
in the after-supper darkness,
rest-happy from the long workday.

GREEN RIVER (1991)

Ghosts in the Carpet

Aunt Pearlie draped her rug across
the fence as though raising a tent
or effigy of her parlor,
and taking up the old shovel
handle slammed the heavy vestment
until it smoked, until it
puffed cloud after cloud out across
the weeds, settling on flowerbeds,
garden rows, the dusts of winter
and the leaner spring, the sheddings
and fibers, the fine silts of human
habitation caught between
the weft threads, motes and tiny crusts,
microscopic morsels, little
prisms fogging over the wet
summer vegetation as she
swung and swung again, freeing lint
and fine detritus to fade like
phantoms in the hard sun, flogging
away the soil and hair and rust
from the fabric's memory. And
after the rug was bright, the colors
new, she beat still more the patterns
with her ancient stick until they
sparkled and exhaled no more dirt,
but hung pure and breathless, heavy
in the breeze, their ghosts given up.

We Are the Dream of Jefferson

To be rocked to sleep by mountains
equals the rest of heroes.
The great Welshman where he lies in
his blue ridge dreams of our continuing.
Underneath his granite column
on the slope he creates through
the text of his thought these conflicts,
the multiple and possible.
Buried high and deep, attired in
silk and brocade and powdered hair,
he rests on his cold slab and sees
through closed eyes the scope of contrary
landscapes proceeding to the end
of the continent. From his hidden
horizon he not so much orders
as observes and follows out each
unfolding of the fabric, each
minute twist of fiber, warp and
return, while the pasture hills roll
on to highway and crowded mall,
city and refinery, slum and
harbor, to the Rockies, to space.
His narrative curiosity
enjoys the process day by day,
his thought a voice that declares
and echoes through mountains, beyond
rivers, as the expeditions
touch alien airs, stranger shores,
in the telling out of the present
through all its painful dissonance.

Appleglow

All was rotten with late summer.
Ida's dahlias leaned to the grass
and burst like supernovas, fat
petals scattering to rust. Weeds
and grass were heavy with seeds and
in the orchard every tree
showed the avoirdupois of harvest.
Fallen apples were the only
sign of last night's storm-epiphany.
All seemed tuned to intoxicating
distances. Even the shade had
the radiance of fruit, yellow
leaves, and butterflies and bees sparked
the afternoon with sulfur. Day
was a white locomotive. To
escape the heat and Sunday glare
we climbed, Harold and I, not the
mountain but Aunt Ida's apple.
Each braced in a fork and picked
the biggest Golden Delicious,
and bit its foaming honey, then
reached for a purple grape on one
side, a red one on the other,
in the tree's interior shade.
Each berry broke like the cool of
deep space on the tongue. All afternoon
we perched there while Mt. Rushmores of
cloud were carved above and lost. When
we came down it was damp in grass
and shadows made a different world
as the late sun feasted red on trees
and grass and appleglow of peaks.

Earache

The red wind in my ear would not lay.
I listened through the tunnel of pain
as they carried me pacing the hallway

and in the room where the fireplace ran
cold air. The close ceiling smothered me.
The rose syrup they poured in hurt more than

the night chill. The house throbbed harshly
to the beat behind my eyes, night after night
all winter, till they called a group finally

and chain-prayed in a circle, saying hot
words over my head, each kneeling in turn.
The ache shrank down its nerve and was quiet.

The air stretched cool as whispering vines,
revealing its shifty musics and designs.

Subduction

The hills are young and the river
of earth itself passes away,
ashes to ashes, fire to fire,

in rubble tide and boiling tremor
spread from cracks in the hot rift clay.
The hills are young and the river

feeds on new mud from the interior,
as land pushes the land away,
ashes to ashes, fire to fire.

Skull plate on skull plate grinds over
rock and continent, then gives way.
The hills are young and the river

slips beneath the wrinkled shore
sliding back to the womb each day,
ashes to ashes, fire to fire.

The many tongues of earth that pour
back into the birth country say
the hills are young, and the river,
ashes to ashes, fire to fire.

TOPSOIL ROAD (2000)

Topsoil Road

The first wagon trace into hills
took no grading. A few trees cut
and brush knocked down or pushed aside,
the route went right across the ridge
and down along the branch. Wheels sliced
into leaves and tore the humus,
banged on roots and rocks and ground
the topsoil in the rush toward
the horizon, to step into
the future the West pulled them to.
No creek or rocky shelf could stall
such exhilaration. Their passion
poured in floods along the ruts as
oxen bawled and stabbed the dirt with
hooves and horses tamped the gravel.
When it rained every track became
a runnel, became a run or
ditch becoming a gully in
yellow clay and red, the wash burned
deep in wet weather reaching to
subsoil and bedrock and making
new horizons in dust as traffic
plowed and plowed again thaw furrows
and puddle holes, until the road
was more pit than passageway, more
obstacle than access, and yet
another must be found to soothe
the unbearable urge to stride
beyond and back, as eros fed
erosion and wander vision
vanished quick as snow in May.

Wild Peavines

I have never understood how
the mountains when first seen by hunters
and traders and settlers were covered
with peavines. How could every cove
and clearing, old field, every
opening in the woods and even
understories of deep woods
be laced with vines and blossoms in
June? They say the flowers were so thick
the fumes were smothering. They tell
of shining fogs of bees above
the sprawling mess and every bush
and sapling tangled with tender
curls and tresses. I don't see how
it was possible for wild peas
to take the woods in shade and deep
hollows and spread over cliffs in
hanging gardens and choke out other
flowers. It's hard to believe the creek
banks and high ledges were that bright.
But hardest of all is to see
how such profusion, such overwhelming
lushness and lavish, could vanish,
so completely disappear that
you must look through several valleys
to find a sprig or strand of wild
peavine curling on a weedstalk
like some word from a lost language
once flourishing on every tongue.

Squatting

The men in rural places when
they stop to talk and visit will
not stand, for that would make it seem
they're in a rush. Nor will they sit
on ground that might be cold or wet.
Instead they squat with dignity
on heels close to the ground and chat
for hours. And while they tell and answer,
or listen, hunkered out of wind,
they draw with sticks in dirt a map
to illustrate a story or
show evidence for argument.
They sketch out patterns, write on dirt
and doodle vague arithmetic,
who never will take up a pen
on page or slate or canvas. They
will absentmindedly make shapes
and figures of their reveries
and rub them out again complete
to give their art no status of
attention in the casual toss
of discourse, open forum of
community, out there on bare
familiar ground where generations
have squatted, called it ownership.

Care

On a cold morning when our grits,
oatmeal, cream of wheat, were dragon hot,
Daddy would take the threatening plates
out to the back porch and blow at

the smoking porridge. He would pant
the steam away and huff until
we laughed at his choo-chooing chant
to drive away the haunt, expel

the fire ghosts that stung our tongues.
We'd wait for him to bring the dishes
back exorcized by his lungs'
performance of burning frenzies,

by the low notes of his breath-fit,
by the owl calls that hushed heat.

Mowing

A summer-long ritual for my father.
Half-dancing and half-rowing into a weed bank,
he gripped the handles of the snath
and swung, beginning high and back, and followed
through, running the blade true
to the ground and then up to winnow
away the cut ends. Snakes and field mice
and my mother's flowers got beheaded
in his rage to mow, and pokeweeds, briars
around the pasture, were subdued to his measure.
He even cut the shoulders of the public road,
exposing beer cans and bags of trash,
and once each season cleaned off the churchyard
and cemetery acre. Mowing met his first requirements:
solitude and no monetary gain. As he swung
he must have seen the heads of neighbors,
deacons, wife and son, topple
and the stubble bleed, for their intrusion
on his long reverie. That blade,
a wide wing of metal, tempered in Czechoslovakia,
soared around and back, making its deadly time
regular as a pendulum, touching its flame
with a hiss to the green stampede.
But there was no end, except frost, to the siege
of tender growth. Suddenly he'd stop
and, holding the scythe upright, take the stone
from his hip pocket and whet the blade brilliant,
spit on his hands and return to the lone war.
I see him there now, wading in rampant vines,
turning quick as a matador in overalls and wrecked hat,
reaching back with his instrument to let
the next wave of summer plunge past and wilt.

Polishing the Silver

Even kept inside its closet
the family tea set, candlestick,
will darken in a year, the brightwork
clouding and smudged with soot

oxygen leaves tasting silver
through months of still and darkness.
We bring the stuff to the terrace
and the polish cream in its jar

and rub away the smoke to find
the mirror flesh original
reflecting us in the ritual,
scrubbing till the heirloom's new and

perfect, glitters as when beaten
and brought back from Charleston over
muddy trail and swollen river
and kept hidden like a weapon.

Family Bible

The leather of the book is soft
and black as that of Grandma's purse,
brought west by horse and wagon, kept
on mantel shelf and closet plank.
The red dye on the edge has faded.
The marriages recorded, births
and deaths set down in pencil and
in many inks and hands, with names
and middle names and different dates
and spellings scrawled in berry juice
that looks like ancient blood. And blood
is what the book's about, the blood
of sacrifice, the blood of Lamb,
two testaments of blood, and blood
of families set in names to show
the course and merging branches, roots
of fluid in your veins this moment.
You open crackly pages thin
as film of river birch and read
the law of blood and soar of blood
in print of word and print of thumb.

Chicken Scratches

Between packed clay of the center
yard and the weeds and shrubbery,
dirt has been raked and scored, crumbs
drying to meal. Some stylus might
have cut the surface and made
a scrawled hand, the little troughs
intersecting, the scabs of crust
picked loose and fresh-stirred mica
signaling around the water can
and boxwoods and dust-holed bank.
The yard deserted, they seem some
funny ogham fading its script
of quest, where the old cluckers raked
back with one claw and then another,
pecked at seeds and grubs and worm eggs
too fine for bigger eyes to catch
among the chalks and gritty signs,
the incunabula of morning.

Harvest Sink

The quills and pens of summer, pipes
and hollow bones, now shine out to
the edge of golden clouds. The wheat
rolls yellow as the coins of woods.
Where now are the hidden valleys
of rain, covert ditches, the shades
of rusts and mildews, smuts and molds
of early summer? Dry clouds tower
in other brightness. Flames spring out
of corn, from vetch and sicklepod,
thistle. The milk of hay is dust.
The little sugarcanes and money
of grass are gritted roughage. Now
every fat weed has gone to harvest.
The sky is still as farthest mountain.

History's Madrigal

When fiddle makers and dulcimer
makers look for best material they
prefer old woods, not just seasoned
but antique, aged, like timbers out
of condemned buildings and poles of
attics and broken furniture
from attics. When asked, they will say
the older wood has sweeter, more
mellow sounds, makes truer and deeper
music, as if the walnut or
cherry, cedar or maple, as
it aged, stored up the knowledge of
passing seasons, the cold and thaw,
whine of storm, bird call and love
moan, news of wars and mourning, in
its fibers, in the sparkling grain,
to be summoned and released by
the craftsman's hands and by careful
fingers on the strings' vibration
decades and generations after
that, the memory and wisdom of
wood delighting air as century
speaks to century and history
dissolves history across the long
and tangled madrigal of time.

The Grain of Sound

A banjo maker in the mountains,
when looking out for wood to carve
an instrument, will walk among
the trees and knock on trunks. He'll hit
the bark and listen for a note.
A hickory makes the brightest sound;
the poplar has a mellow ease.
But only straightest grain will keep
the purity of tone, the sought-
for depth that makes the licks sparkle.
A banjo has a shining shiver.
Its twangs will glitter like the light
on splashing water, even though
its face is just a drum of hide
of cow, or cat, or even skunk.
The hide will magnify the note,
the sad of honest pain, the chill
blood-song, lament, confession, haunt,
as tree will sing again from root
and vein and sap and twig in wind
and cat will moan as hand plucks nerve,
picks bone and skin and gut and pricks
the heart as blood will answer blood
and love begins to knock along the grain.

Honey

Only calmness will reassure
the bees to let you rob their hoard.
Any sweat of fear provokes them.
Approach with confidence, and from
the side, not shading their entrance.
And hush smoke gently from the spout
of the pot of rags, for sparks will
anger them. If you go near bees
every day they will know you.
And never jerk or turn so quick
you excite them. If weeds are trimmed
around the hive they have access
and feel free. When they taste your smoke
they fill themselves with honey and
are laden and lazy as you
lift the lid to let in daylight.
No bee full of sweetness wants to
sting. Resist greed. With the top off
you touch the fat gold frames, each cell
a hex perfect as a snowflake,
a sealed relic of sun and time
and roots of many acres fixed
in crystal-tight arrays, in rows
and lattices of sweeter latin
from scattered prose of meadow, woods.

June Bug

With a thread on his claw I flew
my June bug like a model plane
around the hot pasture. It dipped
and circled and looped above me
as I ran to find wind. Over
the steaming grass it dove like
a jeweled fighter tethered to my
finger, then disappeared into
the swarm of its own kind in clover
and indigo. I had to pull it
back to our play, but let it lead
me in compensation over
the meadow. As it swung close to
my ear I felt the tiny wind
from its wings like a love whisper.